GRACE
Breakthrough
STUDY GUIDE

This Study Guide Belongs to...

BILL GIOVANNETTI
with
ADALINE COLEMAN

GRACE

Breakthrough

Exploding the Lies That Wound Your Confidence and Joy

Endurant Press

GRACE BREAKTHROUGH STUDY GUIDE: EXPLODING THE LIES THAT WOUND YOUR CONFIDENCE AND JOY

Copyright © 2016 Bill Giovannetti

All rights reserved. Neither this book nor any portion thereof may be reproduced or used in any manner whatsoever without the express written permission of the publisher except for the use of brief quotations in a book review. No part of this work may be scanned, uploaded, or distributed via the Internet or any other means, electronic or print, without the publisher's express written permission.

Printed in the United States of America

First Printing, 2016

Endurant Press (www.endurantpress.com)

ISBN Print edition: 978-0-9836812-9-8

All Scripture quotations, unless otherwise indicated, are taken from the New King James Version (R). Copyright © 1982 by Thomas Nelson, Inc. Used by permission. All rights reserved. Scripture quotations marked NLT are taken from the *Holy Bible*, New Living Translation, copyright © 1996, 2004. Used by permission of Tyndale House Publishers, Inc, Wheaton, Illinois 60189. All rights reserved. Scripture quotations marked KJV are taken from the King James Version of the Bible, public domain. Scripture quotations marked NIV are taken from The Holy Bible, New International Version® NIV® Copyright © 1973, 1978, 1984, 2011 by Biblica,Inc.TM. Used by permission. All rights reserved worldwide.

Names have been changed, details have been altered, and persons or events have been made into composites to protect the identity of individuals or organizations referred to herein. Any resemblance to any persons, living or dead is coincidental.

The fonts Ardeco and Cinzel are licensed under the SIL Open Font License, Version 1.1. Used by permission. The font LibelSuit is used by permission under Fontspring EULA 1.6.0. The font Caladea is used by permission under Apache License 2.0.

About the Authors

Dr. Bill Giovannetti serves as senior pastor of Neighborhood Church in Redding, CA, and teaches at A.W. Tozer Theological Seminary. He enjoys life surrounded by snow-capped peaks and pristine forests, along with his wife, Margi, and their kids, Josie and J.D. A popular speaker and author, this is Bill's 6th book. To find out more, visit www.PastorBillG.com.

Adaline Coleman serves as Executive Pastor at Windy City Community Church in Chicago where she has been on staff for 22 years. She holds an M.A.R. from Trinity Evangelical Divinity School where she also served as Dean of Women. Her ministry passions include teaching the Word of God and helping the local church fulfill the Great Commission. She enjoys life with her husband, Rob, and loves kayaking, biking and watching football! Her children, Zac and Meg, are the pride of her days.

CONTENTS

How to Use This Study Guide

Intro: Breaking Through // 7

1. The Grace Breakthrough // 12
2. The Gospel Breakthrough // 19
3. The Security Breakthrough // 24
4. The Identity Breakthrough // 31
5. The Rest Breakthrough // 38
6. The Freedom Breakthrough // 44
7. The Maturity Breakthrough // 50
8. The Confidence Breakthrough // 56
9. The Mission Breakthrough // 62
10. Top Ten Grace Breakthroughs // 68

Bonus Chapters

1. Grace in the Gospels // 73
2. Grace in the Gospels, part 2 // 76
3. Grace in the Gospels, part 3 // 85
4. How to Be Saved // 103

Introduction

HOW TO USE THIS STUDY GUIDE

Purpose

When the light of God's grace first dawns upon a person, it can feel like waking up from a dream. At first there's disorientation, then rejection, then a spiritual wrestling match, and finally a warm embrace.

Hopefully.

Nobody in Scripture came to grace easily. Some fought it, like Paul. Others longed to turn back to bondage, like Israel in the wilderness. Still others simply couldn't get it, like the disciples of Jesus. In each case, grace caused trauma to the status quo.

Why?

Because for the natural mind, the status quo is a web of lies spun by the father of lies.

> But even if our gospel is veiled, it is veiled to those who are perishing, whose minds the god of this age has blinded, who do not believe, lest the light of the gospel of the glory of Christ, who is the image of God, should shine on them. (2 Corinthians 4:3, 4)

The purpose of *Grace Breakthrough,* and of this Study Guide, is to shine the light of Scripture into the grace-blindspots of our souls.

What are the lies we believe about God?

What are the lies we believe about ourselves?

What are the lies we believe about life in this fallen world?

These lies worm deep inside our hearts. They latch onto our tender spirit. They create long-lasting wounds. They nestle in, like Smaug in his mountain of gold. We can forget they exist.

Until there's a disturbance, a frustration, or a need. Then the lies we believe become the kiss of death to our confidence and joy.

You need to pierce the devil's lies in your life. Those lies won't disappear quietly. You need the trauma of a grace breakthrough.

As you open your heart and mind to the truths in *Grace Breakthrough* and in this Study Guide, my prayer is that God will explode the lies that wound your confidence and joy.

How It's Organized

This Study Guide follows a one-chapter-per-week format. Each week offers four parts. Each part offers questions to answer and verses to study. Dig through each part over the course of the week. At the end of each chapter, you'll find a suggestion for the weekend—something to think about or watch for based on that chapter. You'll also find discussion questions for your small group or family.

If it's too much, don't worry. Nobody is grading you, and there's no rush. God will guide you, and his Spirit will mentor you, as you apply your heart to God's truth in Scripture.

Blast through quickly, or stroll through at a leisurely pace, it's your call.

Make it Your Own

Here are some different ideas on how you can use this Study Guide:

1. Privately, to assist in your own personal reflection and growth.
2. With your spouse, fiancé, or significant friend in your life. Work together through each chapter, and pray for one another.
3. As a family quiet time, meditation, or devotional.
4. With your small group, Bible study, or Sunday School class.
5. On a retreat: men, women, singles, couples, seniors, young adults, students. Select a few chapters and dig deep.
6. For a preaching/teaching series in your church or Bible class.

7. In a Celebrate Recovery group, or other Recovery Group. Those of us struggling with hurts, habits, and hang-ups, have been radically transformed by the principles in this book.
8. To help anyone rise above the traumas of a difficult past. Breaking through the lies is a life-changing part of your healing.
9. For use in any classroom or home-school setting.
10. For a college dorm fellowship group, or campus ministry.

Some chapters have more questions than others. If at any point it feels like too much work, just stop. Back off. Don't be legalistic with yourself or with your group. So what if you just do the odd numbered questions, or the even numbered chapters? Nobody will be hurt. You can always come back, review the book, and finish a year or two from now.

I pray that God will use these discussions to blast through a lifetime of messed up lies. I pray deep healing for the wounds of a distorted conscience, a warped view of God, and a dysfunctional view of self. I pray God will set you on the beautiful, real, sustainable ground of truth – where the amazing thing called grace is the heart of everything.

Bill Giovannetti

Introduction

Grace Breakthrough

PART 1 → "But none of these things move me; nor do I count my life dear to myself, so that I may finish my race with joy, and the ministry which I received from the Lord Jesus, to testify to the gospel of the grace of God." (Acts 20:24)

The Mother of All the Devil's Lies
GOD IS LESS THAN HE SAYS HE IS.

---

1. Why did you pick up this book? Did someone give it to you? What do you think the giver might have been thinking?

> "THE ONLY WAY GRACE GETS THROUGH IS BY BREAKING THROUGH."

2. The title of book we're studying is *Grace Breakthrough: Exploding the Lies That Wound Your Confidence and Joy.* From the title, what assumptions do you think guided the book? What goals might have guided Bill?

3. What does Jesus say about the devil's dirty tricks in John 8:43-44?

4. Why might "exploding" be the right action for the lies that lie buried in the foundations of our heart?

 **PART 2**   Sanctify them by Your word. Your word is truth. John 17:1

1. A famous pastor from an earlier generation said, "The ultimate test of our spirituality is the measure of our amazement at the grace of God" (D. Martyn Lloyd-Jones). How do you think most people measure their spirituality?

2. What does your attitude toward grace tell you about your spiritual life? Why might it be the best measure of a person's spirituality?

3. Bill suggests that the Mother of All the Devil's Lies is this: "God is less than he says he is." Where might you find this in Scripture? Do you agree? Disagree? How might all other spiritual lies flow out of this one?

PART 3 → Your word I have hidden in my heart, / That I might not sin against You! (Psalm 119:11).

1. Think through the description of grace on the right. What parts of this description surprise you? Raise questions for you? What parts might you change?

2. How are people reverse polarized? What can this do to our view of grace?

"We've too often demoted grace to anything but the tough, exacting, profound, complex, interlocking web of ultimate truths that give meaning and depth to our existence."

3. Bill has described grace as "scandalous." What might make grace feel scandalous to people?

PART 4 For the word of God is living and powerful, and sharper than any two-edged sword, piercing even to the division of soul and spirit, and of joints and marrow, and is a discerner of the thoughts and intents of the heart. (Hebrews 4:12)

1. In Hebrews 4:12, what implement is used to describe the Word of God? Knowing that our hearts are hardened by the Fall, why does this make sense?

2. Who bears the burden of your grace breakthrough? Why?

WEEKEND Look for grace. In the church you attend, in the songs you sing, in the sermon you hear, in the restful times with family and friends; list the references and pictures and illustrations of grace—that you hear, that you receive, that you give, that you live.

DISCUSS 1. Why might the Devil's agenda be for us to believe that God is less than he says he is?

2. What impact would a small God have on a person's life?

3. What example did Bill give of reverse polarization? What was the problem? What was the effect? What was the solution? Why is this concept important in a book about grace?

4. God the Grandmother or God the Big Meanie... Which mischaracterization have you most believed God to be? Which do you see in the people/culture/world around you? Why do you think people move to these false ideas?

> ### Intro Chapter Prayer
>
> Gracious Father,
>
> Bring me to a place where your grace so fills my horizon that the devil's death-dealing lies are all crowded out. Teach me to believe that you are who you say you are — that you are immeasurably better to me than I can ask or think.
>
> Break through whatever lies I believe about you. Pierce the dark night of my soul with the dawn of Calvary's love. Open my eyes to see never-failing streams of abundant grace all around. And create in me the confidence of a firstborn child of a Great King.
>
> Through Christ, the fountain of all grace, I pray,
>
> Amen.

Chapter 1

The Grace Breakthrough

PART 1 — For you know the grace of our Lord Jesus Christ, that though He was rich, yet for your sakes He became poor, that you through His poverty might become rich. (2 Corinthians 8:9)

BIG LIE #1
I'VE GOT GRACE ALL FIGURED OUT.

---

1. Think through how 2 Corinthians 8:9 describes grace: Who is it from and through? What did He do? What does this actually mean? For whose sake? What is the result?

2. Common problem: "Most of God's children limp beneath their true riches in grace." How true is this? How true is it of you?

3. What are some differences between *believing* and *feeling* the truth of grace? One a scale of 1 (low) to 10 (high), to what degree would you say your theology has healed your psychology? Comment.

> "GRACE THEOLOGY NEEDS TO BECOME GRACE PSYCHOLOGY.
> GRACE CAN BECOME A
> DEEP-ROOTED,
> SCRIPTURE-BASED,
> TROUBLE-HARDENED,
> INSTINCTIVE
> WAY OF TAKING ON EVERY DAY BY THE POWER OF THE LOVE OF GOD."

4. Re-phrase each part of this goal in your own words: Grace can become a...

deeply-rooted...

Scripture-based...

trouble-hardened...

instinctive way...

of taking on every day...

by the power of the love of God.

PART 2

> But even if our gospel is veiled, it is veiled to those who are perishing, whose minds the god of this age has blinded, who do not believe, lest the light of the gospel of the glory of Christ, who is the image of God, should shine on them. (2 Corinthians 4:3,4)

1. Bill suggests that "Nobody in the Bible ever understood grace without a breakthrough." Agree or Disagree? Why?

2. If this is true, why do you think it's true? Why must breaking through to grace include a measure of trauma?

3. To what degree do you feel you need this level of transformation? How much do you want it?

4. What does Ephesians 4:18 say about our resistance to grace?

> *...having their understanding darkened, being alienated from the life of God, because of the ignorance that is in them, because of the blindness of their heart...*

PART 3 — "If you're defeated emotionally by dysfunctions Christ has defeated spiritually, you need a breakthrough."

1. When people think of grace, they often think of God, or the Cross, or of a simple leniency on the part of God. *Grace Breakthrough* argues for a much deeper concept of grace. Bill suggests that most of our personal and emotional breakdown happen because we're deficient in grace.

Agree or Disagree? Why?

2. How blind to your own need for grace would you say you have been? What kinds of breakthroughs have you had? When? Where? Describe the moments, if you can.

3. Why do WHINY people need a grace breakthrough?

4. Why might ANXIOUS people need a grace breakthrough?

5. Why might JUDGMENTAL people need a grace breakthrough?

6. Draw an X on each scale below to indicate how you see yourself.

Whiny -- **Thankful**
Anxious -- **Relaxed**
Judgmental -- **Forgiving**

PART 4

1. As this chapter outlines the kinds of people who need a breakthrough, Bill suggests what each type of person is missing. They are "out of touch" with something. Quickly scan through the chapter, and complete this chart.

TYPE OF PEOPLE	EMOTIONALLY OUT OF TOUCH WITH...
1. Whiny People	Your blessings as a child of God.
2. Anxious People	
3. Judgmental People	
4. Insecure People	
5. Guilty People	
6. Overwhelmed People	
7. Smug People	

2. Draw an X on each scale below to indicate how you see yourself.

Insecure--**Confident**
Guilty---**Forgiven**
Overwhelmed---**Solid**
Smug---**Humble**

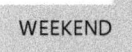

Try to spot Grace Deficit Disorder throughout the weekend, but don't judge people for it. Look for evidence of the seven kinds of people in this chapter. Really notice how so many of our struggles can be traced to a deficit of grace—that is, to low thoughts of our Heavenly Father, our position in grace, and God's faithful provision in our lives.

DISCUSS

1. What are most people's top misconceptions of God? How do most people view him in ways that are the opposite of what the Bible says?
2. How do people harbor misconceptions about themselves? Do more people think higher than they ought to think or lower? What does Romans 12:3 say about this?
3. What are some ways people be deficient in grace and not even know it?
4. What do you think comes to mind for most people when they hear the word *grace*? How might these thoughts diverge from what the Bible says?

Grace Breakthrough Prayer

O Lord,

Please pull off my blinders. Awaken my heart to your love. Deliver me from the lie that I've got grace all figured out. Show me oceans of your love I have yet to explore.

Where I am whiny, make me thankful. Where I am anxious, make me brave. Where I am judgmental, make me compassionate and full of merciful love. Strengthen me in my insecurities. Deliver me from guilt and shame. When the floods of life overwhelm me, be my rock and hold me tightly. And whatever spirit of smugness I may show, Lord humble me that I might experience the grace that's always there.

Lord Jesus, live through me.

I pray in your name alone,

Amen.

Chapter 2

The Gospel Breakthrough

PART 1 → For I am not ashamed of the gospel of Christ, for it is the power of God to salvation for everyone who believes, for the Jew first and also for the Greek. (Romans 1:16)

BIG LIE #2

GOD WILL COMMIT HIMSELF TO ME WHEN I COMMIT MYSELF TO HIM WITH ENOUGH DETERMINATION.

---

1. Why would the author call this a lie? On a scale of 1-10, how good are most people at following through on commitments? How would you rate yourself?

2. Is the Gospel more about your commitment to God or God's commitment to you? Why?

3. Consider two definitions of "commitment:" 1). Dedicating yourself to proper performance and effort. 2). Entrusting something or someone to the performance and effort of Another. Read 2 Timothy 1:12. Which definition does Paul have in mind? Why?

PART 2 In Him you also trusted, after you heard the word of truth, the gospel of your salvation; in whom also, having believed, you were sealed with the Holy Spirit of promise, who is the guarantee of our inheritance until the redemption of the purchased possession, to the praise of His glory. (Ephesians 1:13, 14)

1. According to Ephesians 1:13, 14, after you heard the gospel of your salvation, what did you do next?

2. What did God, by the Holy Spirit, do to you next? What do you think that means?

3. What does it mean to trust someone? What does it mean to trust in Jesus Christ?

PART 3-4 For I delivered to you first of all that which I also received: that Christ died for our sins according to the Scriptures, and that He was buried, and that He rose again the third day according to the Scriptures. (1 Corinthians 15:1-4)

Chapter 2, The Gospel Breakthrough, covers five "indispensable facts" of the Gospel. Fill in the chart on the next page with some major notes, summaries, or reactions to these facts.

Which ones stood out for you? Which ones did you struggle with? Are these truths new? Debatable? Dig in to the gospel of grace and let God's Spirit and Word guide you. Take a couple of days to do this if needed.

Indispensable Facts	Summary, Comments, Reaction
1. Definition	
2. Nature	
3. Core	
4. Response	
5. Distortions	1. Give your life to Christ. 2. Follow Christ. 3. Ask Jesus into your heart. 4. Count the cost. 5. Make Jesus your Lord and Master.

> No surer test can be applied to any truth claiming to be the gospel than this: *What does it make of Christ Jesus and him crucified?* Is he part of it, or is he all? Where is your hope for eternity?

WEEKEND → As you go through your weekend, especially at church, really pay special attention to the Cross and the death of Christ. How much do we emphasize this "Ground Zero" of our salvation? Do we hear about it, think about it, sing about it, and teach about it enough?

DISCUSS → 1. Look up the following Bible verses and discuss their laser beam focus on the Cross. Why do you think this is so important? How well do you think most Christians and churches reflect this priority?

1 Corinthians 2:2

Galatians 6:14

1 Corinthians 1:18

1 Corinthians 1:23

2. Discuss how the Gospel can never make God's commitment to you DEPEND UPON your commitment to God without becoming bad news. Discuss how the Gospel can reverse that and make your commitment to God a *response* to God's commitment to you through Christ and his Cross.

Gospel Breakthrough Prayer

Gracious Lord,

How I thank you for this beautiful gospel of grace. Pure grace, nothing but grace. I worship you, Lord Jesus, for your death on Calvary's Cross. There, you washed my sins away. There, you shattered the barrier that kept me from God. Whatever punishment, condemnation, guilt, and shame my sins deserved, you accomplished there. When you cried, "It is finished," you cemented this gospel of grace in place for all the ages long.

I bless you for the Cross. And I thank you that you did not place salvation out of reach of the humblest person who believes. Faith alone in Christ alone.

What a gospel! And what a Savior.

Lord Jesus, I confess you as my only hope for life, for eternity, for forgiveness, and for adoption into your family. I am so grateful for the people who first shared your good news with me.

I pray that others will find the same treasure that I found when you found me.

In Christ's grace,

Amen

CHAPTER 3

The Security Breakthrough

PART 1 — For He Himself has said, "I will never leave you nor forsake you." So we may boldly say: "The Lord is my helper; I will not fear. What can man do to me?" (Hebrews 13:5b, 6)

BIG LIE #3
IF I DON'T STAY FAITHFUL TO GOD, HE WON'T STAY FAITHFUL TO ME.

---

1. Finish the "Big Idea" from *Grace Breakthrough*, p. 52: "God himself bears all the burden to..." How new is this to you? How difficult or easy is it for you to believe?

2. Have you known anyone who has gotten "saved" over and over again? Why might that happen? Is it even possible? Why or why not?

3. Look up the following verses, and make some notes about the permanence of your salvation.

Romans 8:38,39

John 10:27-29

Philippians 1:6

 So when Jesus had received the sour wine, He said, "It is finished!" And bowing His head, He gave up His spirit. (John 19:30)

1. How might insecurities in a relationship with God spill over into other insecurities in a person's life?

2. This chapter explores three key areas of emotional insecurity, and links them to how we feel about our security in Christ. Take a few moments to make some notes about each of these areas and your own life.

Abandonment	
Acceptance	
Appearance	

3. When Jesus, from the Cross, cried out, "It is Finished!" what do you think he meant?

4. Take a moment to pray over each potential insecurity for yourself and for some people you love and care about.

PART 3

Blessed be the God and Father of our Lord Jesus Christ, who according to His abundant mercy has begotten us again to a living hope through the resurrection of Jesus Christ from the dead, to an inheritance incorruptible and undefiled and that does not fade away, reserved in heaven for you, who are kept [guarded, shielded] by the power of God through faith for salvation ready to be revealed in the last time. (1 Peter 1:3-5)

1. Draw an X through the forces in your life that cannot defeat God and cannot destroy your salvation:

Sin	**Satan**	**Struggles**
Death	**Enemies**	**Mistakes**
My Past	**My Shame**	**My Secrets**
In-laws	**People I've let down**	**My ex-**
Lack of integrity	**Weaknesses**	**Addiction**
Success	**Riches**	**Poverty**
Imperfections	**Pride**	**Loneliness**

2. Imagine a strong chain that connects you to God and his salvation. Consider this question: *if your eternal destiny depends upon the strength of that chain, how many links of the chain do you want God himself to forge, and how many links do you want to forge?* Explain your answer.

3. From what you know of God and the Bible, does his faithfulness to you depend on his own character or on yours? Why? What does Psalm 119:89, 90 say about this?

PART 4

You shall no longer be termed Forsaken, Nor shall your land any more be termed Desolate; But you shall be called Hephzibah, and your land Beulah; For the LORD delights in you, And your land shall be married. (Isaiah 62:4)

1. What does Hephzibah mean (p. 63)?

2. What does Beulah mean (p. 63)?

3. In the space below, rewrite Isaiah 62:4 in the first person (using the words I and ME), and try to insert your own name.

> I shall no longer be termed "Forsaken," Nor shall my...

WEEKEND — Try this experiment. Each day this weekend, when you wake up, and before you go to bed, read Hebrews 14:6 out loud a couple of times. Try reading it boldly, and try reading it timidly. Which makes more sense?

> FOR HE HIMSELF HAS SAID, "I WILL NEVER LEAVE YOU NOR FORSAKE YOU." SO WE MAY BOLDLY SAY: "THE LORD IS MY HELPER; I WILL NOT FEAR. WHAT CAN MAN DO TO ME?"
> (HEBREWS 13:5B, 6)

DISCUSS

1. Why might people be naturally opposed to the teaching of Eternal Security?
2. What is the relationship between the power of the Cross and the security of your salvation?
3. What good is a salvation that doesn't permanently save?
4. Where do you struggle and how does the security of grace impact

Abandonment? (who has left you? Or was never there?)

Acceptance Issues? (who rejected you or never truly accepted you?)

Appearance Issues? (what is "wrong" with the way you look? Why is it wrong?)

Security Breakthrough Prayer

Almighty God,

You took hold of my hand the day you saved me, and you have never let me go. You will never let me go. And you can never let me go, because you promised to walk me all the way home to you.

Lord, break through my insecurities. When I worry about your love for me, hold me close. When fears of the future gather on the horizon, tower over them. When I question my salvation, assure me by your Spirit and your Word. When I feel the need to hide from you, wipe it away, and help me believe your invitation to come boldly to you.

I rest all my anxieties in you, and I claim by faith the utter, eternal, and irrevocable security in which I stand by grace alone.

Through Christ's Great Love,

Amen.

Chapter 4

The Identity Breakthrough

PART 1

Therefore we were buried with Him through baptism into death, that just as Christ was raised from the dead by the glory of the Father, even so we also should walk in newness of life. For if we have been united together in the likeness of His death, certainly we also shall be in the likeness of His resurrection. (Romans 6:4, 5)

BIG LIE #4

I MUST STAY BUSY FOR JESUS TO PROVE MYSELF TO GOD AND OTHERS.

NOTE: This chapter has 5 parts in the study guide.

1. Have you ever heard a "yes-but" to grace? Have you ever spoken or thought one? Why do you think most people are so quick to add qualifiers and disclaimers to grace?

2. When Christians behave badly, is the problem too much grace or too little? What do you think of Bill's assessment that unholy behavior stems from Grace Deficit Disorder—too little grace in a person's life and heart?

PART 2

> But by the grace of God I am what I am, and His grace toward me was not in vain; but I labored more abundantly than they all, yet not I, but the grace of God which was with me. (1 Corinthians 15:10)

1. "People act out of who they are." Can you give an example when you witnessed this truth in action?

2. Using *Grace Breakthrough,* finish the five steps of an Identity Breakthrough.

1	People act out of who they are.
2	You've been...
3	The labels you embrace create...
4	Grace rehabs the....
5	Grace rehabs your identity by...

3. Comment on the logical flow of these five steps. Does this make sense to you? Why or why not?

PART 3 ▶ THE MORE STRESSED I FEEL, THE HARDER IT IS TO BELIEVE THAT WHAT GOD SAYS ABOUT ME IS TRUE.

1. What are some forces or life experiences that can wound a person's sense of self?

2. Why do you think grace rehabs the identity first? Why is this important for authentic life change?

3. According to legalism, how do people change to become more like Christ? According to grace?

> When your identity rests on grace, nobody can define you. Nobody can defeat you or dominate you..

PART 4

1. What are some differences between how you would normally describe yourself and how God would describe you in Christ? How hard are you working to "prove" your value and worth? Why might you do that?

2. On a scale between these two descriptions, write a T for where your theology is. Write a P for where your psychology is (your mind and your heart). So put a T and a P on each line:

Lost	Found
In darkness	In the light
Alienated	Reconciled
In your sins	Forgiven
Without righteousness	Declared righteous
Condemned	Accepted
Stuck	Redeemed
Unworthy	Fully qualified
Child of wrath	Child of God
Sinner	Saint

3. As you make your Grace Breakthroughs, your psychology begins to catch up with your theology. How would you describe your progress so far?

PART 5 I can do all things through Christ who strengthens me. (Philippians 4:13)

1. Do you think you'll ever get to a point where you are essentially healed from the traumas and losses of your past? To what degree is that even possible?

2. Think about a recent time you were stressed and didn't handle it well. What did you start to say to yourself when the stress started building? What did you say *about* yourself? How did those statements create messed up behavior?

"The more stressed I feel, the harder it is to believe that what God says about me is true."

3. What are 2-4 labels you apply to yourself that simply have to change? Will you pray right now to ask God to peel off those labels? Will you embrace the labels God puts on you in Christ?

4. In your own words, sum up the idea of Union with Christ.

WEEKEND — As you go through your weekend, pray through the list on page 80-81 about who you are in Christ. As you pray, declare to God that you embrace each quality, one by one. Ask God to make them become your real life experience and feeling.

DISCUSS
1. How common is a distorted identity?
2. How does this play into addictions? Dating? Sexuality? Finance? Relationships? Child rearing? Success in school? Success in career? Ministry?
3. If God's children truly saw themselves as God sees them, how might that change their lives?
4. How might that change the world?

Identity Breakthrough Prayer

Father,

I am who you say I am. It's hard to believe it sometimes. I've heard so many different messages through my life. I've received so many heartbreaking labels. The more stressed I feel, the harder it is to believe that what you say about me is true.

But it is true. I take you at your Word. I believe you. My truest self, the real me, has been joined to Christ. I share his name. I share his nature. I share his identity. I am not what other people say I am — I am who you say I am and will be forever.

Thank you for my union with Christ.

Help me to grow deeper and deeper into my truest nature in Christ.

Through My Savior's Name,

CHAPTER 5

The Rest Breakthrough

PART 1 → "Come to Me, all you who labor and are heavy laden, and I will give you rest." (Matthew 11:28)

> **BIG LIE #5**
>
> GOD MAKES ME WRESTLE MY BLESSINGS OUT OF HIM.

1. Read the story of Mary and Martha in Luke 10:38-42. What's your first reaction when Jesus corrects the one who labored and praises the one who "did nothing"? Does it seem fair? If you were Martha, how might you have responded?

2. Have you ever thought that you have to "wrestle" your blessings out of God? Earn them? Deserve them? Strive for them?

3. Comment on the stories of the Sacred Stairs, and the girls who couldn't get into church because they were wearing shorts. What thoughts, feelings, and memories come up for you?

> **PART 2**
>
> *The moral of this story is not the victory of wrestling; it is the victory of clinging.*

1. Define *wrestling* and *clinging* as they are used here.

2. What do you look like when you wrestle with God? What do you look like when you cling to God?

3. How do the ideas of wrestling God and clinging to God reveal themselves in your personal relationship with God?

> God's love is not for sale. God's love is not a prize given to moral winners. It is not a reward for great spiritual performances. God's love flows eternally for his heart. You don't have to wrestle it out of him.

PART 3

"These things I have spoken to you, that in Me you may have peace. In the world you will have tribulation; but be of good cheer, I have overcome the world." (John 16:33)

1. Another way that legalism rears its ugly head is in the statement, "I don't deserve this." When trials and hardships come your way, how do you respond? What do you say about the fairness of God? About what you deserve from him or don't deserve from him?

2. Does God wear you out? Jesus? Church? Christians? Why or why not?

3. Read the following verses and note HOW good works and Christian service are supposed to be done. When good works are done God's way, where does the power come from? Make some notes.

Colossians 1:19

1 Corinthians 15:10

Philippians 2:13

PART 4

1. What do you think Jacob was feeling while he was wrestling God? Do you think he knew it was God?

2. What had to happen for Jacob to give up wrestling? Why do you think God let the wrestling match go on for so long before he finally took drastic action?

3. What does it look like to cling to God? What does Jesus say about this in John 15:5? What does it mean to "abide in Christ?" What does it produce?

> "I AM THE VINE, YOU ARE THE BRANCHES. HE WHO ABIDES IN ME, AND I IN HIM, BEARS MUCH FRUIT; FOR WITHOUT ME YOU CAN DO NOTHING.
> ~JESUS
> (JOHN 15:5)

WEEKEND Look for hurry in your life. Look for times you get worked up and anxious. Rushed. Snippy. Impatient. What are you trying to prove? What do you feel you're losing? How are pent up frustrations making you crazy? When you catch yourself turning hyper, read John 15:4,5 and tell God you will rest your heart in him.

DISCUSS 1. What might be some modern day versions of the Sacred Stairs?

2. Why is there so much teaching that says we have to earn our blessings from God? What does that imply about God? About us?

3. In the story of Mary with Jesus and Martha in the kitchen, how is Mary a model of rest and Martha a model of needless labor? Is there a way to be in the kitchen for Jesus *while resting at the same time?*

4. How is resting in Christ different from laziness or passivity?

Rest Breakthrough Prayer

God,

I'm tired. I'm tired of working. Tired of striving. Tired of trying to prove myself to you. I'm tired of the religious treadmill. Tired of caring what other people think.

Jesus, you said your burden was easy and your yoke was light, but I've turned my relationship with you into a miserable chore.

I'm done with that.

Today, I rest my weary soul in you. Today, I cast the burden of labor onto you and you alone. My job is faith; your job is everything else.

I rest in your character. I rest in your promises. I rest in your provision. I rest in your grace.

I rest in you.

Gratefully, in Christ,

Amen

CHAPTER 6

The Freedom Breakthrough

PART 1 → Delight yourself also in the LORD, And He shall give you the desires of your heart. Commit your way to the LORD, Trust also in Him, And He shall bring it to pass. (Psalm 37:4, 5)

BIG LIE #6

GOD DOESN'T CARE ABOUT WHAT I WANT – WHAT HE WANTS IS ALL THAT MATTERS.

---

1. Why do you think the missionary Bill talked about found it so difficult to express his true wants? What are some possible reasons?

> However, self-denial in and of itself is not a virtue: finding and living truth is. If following God's truth somewhere yields self-denial, so be it. It's the occasional byproduct, not the point, of following God's ways.

2. What's the difference between self-denial as a potential *byproduct* of following God, and self-denial as the *point* of following God? Why is this important?

3. How has following God led to *healthy* self-denial in your life? Give one or two examples if possible. How do you feel about this?

> **PART 2** — "If you abide in Me, and My words abide in you, you will ask what you desire, and it shall be done for you." (John 15:7)

Your heart's deepest desires, when you are tight with God, become a reliable guide to his will for your life.

1. What is your reaction to that statement? Do you agree or disagree? Why?

2. Does it make you afraid, angry, or excited?

3. How might your *surface* desires differ from your *deepest* desires? Which do you think concerns God most? How "in touch" are most people with their surface desires? Their deepest desires?

PART 3

1. Note your comments and reactions to each of the "False Assumptions" discussed in this chapter. What changes, if any, would you make to these statements to make them true?

1. My will and God's will never intersect.	
2. The Christian's will must be "broken."	
3. Christian freedom is just an illusion.	

2. What are some differences between a *broken* will and a *yielded* will? Which expression is a better match for God's expectation of you? Why?

PART 4 — Let us therefore come boldly to the throne of grace, that we may obtain mercy and find grace to help in time of need. (Hebrews 4:16)

> "Love God and do what you really, deeply, passionately want, as much as the choice:
> ☑ keeps your word,
> ☑ obeys the Bible,
> ☑ honors your spouse/family, and
> ☑ keeps you paying your bills."

1. Is this an acceptable standard? Is it biblically acceptable? Does it lower the bar or raise the bar for your life?

2. What other standards would you require in making choices?

3. When you seek your heart's desires, does that mean you will always get them? Will you always get what you want? What does it mean when you don't get the desires of your heart?

> **WEEKEND** — Look for times in your life when you say *yes* when you'd rather say *no*. Is this legit self-denial or is it something else? Are you wimping out on your deeper desires, or are you fulfilling the true requirements of self-giving love? Is it true freedom to continue agreeing to these things? (Remember, there is a place for self-denial – it's a genuine part of love. Just make sure it's not dysfunctional love.)

> **DISCUSS** — 1. Which of the following expressions have you heard taught in Christian circles? Which are valid? Which do you think should be avoided? Why?

Self-denial. Dying to self. Ego annihilation. Crucifying myself. Brokenness. Bearing my cross.

2. Are there ways to frame these expressions so they honor Scripture and your soul? Are there ways to frame them so they are off base and incorrect?
3. How much do people pursue superficial desires at the expense of deep desires? Why does this happen?
4. Read Luke 9:23 where Jesus calls us to deny ourselves. Is he talking about denying our wants, or is it possible he's talking about denying our abilities to save ourselves, and to merit God's favor by our own efforts? Which interpretation seems to fit better with the tone of Scripture? Why?

Freedom Breakthrough Prayer

Dear Lord,

I take back the scepter of my heart. I reclaim my life's throne. You gave me dominion, the devil took it away, and by faith I take it back.

Deliver me from the legalism that says my wants are irrelevant. Forgive me for making you so picky and demanding that I'm afraid to make a choice.

Lord, renew my heart, my mind, and my will. Cause me to want what you want. To desire what you desire. Align my will with yours. Revise the desires of my heart so they perfectly mesh with the desires of your heart for me.

Then open doors that lead me to fulfill those desires. Grant that I would dream your dreams for my life, and have the courage to pursue them. Do all of this by your grace, and through Christ who lives in me.

In His Name,

Amen

CHAPTER 7

The Maturity Breakthrough

 But grow in the grace and knowledge of our Lord and Savior Jesus Christ. To Him be the glory both now and forever. Amen. (2 Peter 3:18)

BIG LIE #7

I'M SAVED, SO I'VE ARRIVED.

---

1. Why is spiritual growth important? How much is it talked about in churches you have attended?

2. Fill in the blanks from page 108.

Let's decode "the Promised Land" into this: *a place in life where you _____ _____ _____ from God, and God receives _____ _____ from you.*

3. List some parallels between the ancient Jews wandering [needlessly] in the wilderness for 40 years, and a person's lack of growth and maturity today.

PART 2

Therefore, since a promise remains of entering His rest, let us fear lest any of you seem to have come short of it. (Hebrews 4:1)

1. Review the "Acres of Diamonds" story. What does it look like in a person's life when they fail to enjoy their riches in Christ and the promises of God? How does that play out?

2. In what ways do you see yourself in the Acres of Diamonds story?

> YOU HAVE BEEN SO ABUNDANTLY SUPPLIED WITH GRACE-POWERS, THAT THERE WILL NEVER BE A CALL OF GOD ON YOUR LIFE TO WHICH YOU NEED TO SAY, "I CAN'T."

3. Cross out the qualities below that don't really apply to you. Circle the ones that do. How might spiritual maturity and growth in grace help you rise above these negative qualities?

Insecurities	Legalism	Bitterness	Addictions
Self-righteousness	Need to correct others	Vengefulness	Negative labels from your past
Temper tantrums	Violence	Deception	Unholiness in habits & thought
Pity parties	Victimhood	Immorality	Narcissism

PART 3

1. Give a brief description of each area of growth (beginning on page 116). Make a few comments about your own progress in each category. Still at the kiddie table or have you moved up?

1	Grow in Grace-Promises	
2	Grow in Grace-Powers	
3	Grow in Grace-Living	
4	Grow in Grace-Victory	

2. Do you see a progression here? Why might this order make sense?

PART 4

> And not only that, but we also glory in tribulations, knowing that tribulation produces perseverance; and perseverance, character; and character, hope. Now hope does not disappoint, because the love of God has been poured out in our hearts by the Holy Spirit who was given to us. (Romans 5:3-5)

1. Before reading *Grace Breakthrough*, did you have a picture in your mind of a "mature Christian?" What did that person look like?

2. How does Bill describe a mature Christian (p. 125)?

3. How has your understanding changed?

4. What are some ways in which *grace* connects with *maturity*?

WEEKEND → Look for signs of maturity or immaturity in different areas of your life this weekend. Family. Dating. Parenting. Work. School. Studies. Emotional maturity. In how you speak. In your emotions, dysfunctions, and instincts. Where are the gaps in your maturity? Where are you strong in maturity? How is Jesus expressing his life and power through you? Where are you hindering that?

DISCUSS → 1. Why do you think Bill says, "When you take in the Word of God, you don't just get information, you also get power"? How does this power relate to spiritual maturity?

2. Can people be active for Jesus while also being spiritually immature? What do you think is God's evaluation of this situation? How does Jesus respond to this in Luke 10:38-42?

3. How familiar are most Christians with the riches of the promises of God? How common is this teaching?

4. In your estimation, what kinds of circumstance cause most Christians to doubt the love of God? How do these doubts spring from immaturity? How might a mature walk with Christ dispel these doubts.

Maturity Breakthrough Prayer

Lord,

Help me grow. I'm tired of the wandering. Tired of the wilderness. And tired of the kiddie table.

I believe you have showered an immense mountain of grace and blessing upon me — you blessed me with infinite treasures the day I was born again.

Now, I want to unwrap those grace-gifts. I want to experience them. I want to rise up to my inheritance. I don't want to walk away from acres of diamonds; I want to collect them, polish them, and enjoy them. You have a Promised Land for me; deliver me from coasting in the wilderness.

Lord, I'm done with the kiddie table. I'm moving on up. I confess I can't do this by my own human strength. So you be my power, dear Lord. You be my strength. Let Christ be formed in me. Let your Holy Scriptures transform my mind. Let the Spirit wield the Sword of the Word with precision and power.

Make me a Caleb, and give me the mountain of grace, where I experience maximum grace from you, and you receive maximum glory from me.

Grow me up, I pray...

In Christ Alone,

Amen.

Chapter 8

The Confidence Breakthrough

PART 1 → Let us therefore come boldly to the throne of grace, that we may obtain mercy and find grace to help in time of need. (Hebrews 4:16)

BIG LIE #8

FEAR KEEPS THE FAITHFUL FAITHFUL.

---

1. What is your response to the idea that "fear keeps the faithful faithful"?

2. What are some ways in which this message is subtly (or blatantly) communicated by Christians, pastors, books, parents, and churches?

3. Bill talks about "a God who simply can't be satisfied no matter how hard I try." How much does your heart resonate with that idea about God? How common do you think this view is among Christians?

> **PART 2** Legalism's germs proliferate in the dank cellars of fear. They thrive in the moisture of an implacable deity – a God who simply can't be satisfied no matter how hard I try.

1. What are the differences between *salvation* and *assurance*? Why did Bill call his experience in the high school gym the "date of his assurance"?

2. How much of a role do guilt and shame play in most Christian's lives? How much should they play?

3. What are some unhealthy areas of fear in your life with God? How does the anti-grace message of legalism feed these fears?

4. Why do *legalism* and *bondage* go hand in hand? How do *grace* and *adoption* pair up?

It is Finished

PART 3 — There is therefore now no condemnation to those who are in Christ Jesus, who do not walk according to the flesh, but according to the Spirit. (Romans 8:1)

1. According to this chapter, what is REPENTANCE? (See pages 133-135.) How does this differ from other definitions you have heard?

2. If you could describe the emotions you feel when you think about God – and about the day you meet him face to face – in one word, what would that word be?

3. What does 1 John 2:28 say about how we feel when we appear before the Lord at his coming. How is this even possible? How does it square with what you feel?

PART 4

1. What does it mean to say that "love keeps the faithful faithful"? Whose love is in view? What does Romans 5:5 say about this?

2. Circle the items that play a role in your life. Put an X through the ones that don't. Pray that God would displace fear in your life with his supernatural, divine love.

Fear of God.	**Fear of abandonment.**
Fear of final judgment.	**Fear of exposure.**
Fear of people's opinions.	**Fear of the disapproving frown.**
Fear of outsider status.	**Fear of death.**
Fear of hell.	**Fear of the devil.**
Fear of your own heart.	**Fear of suffering for those I love.**

3. Jot down some notes about the love God has for you. What is it like? Where does it come from? What can interrupt it? Break it? Nullify it? What role does Jesus play in it? How deeply do you feel it? What are some favorite Bible verses about God's love? Take a while, and really think – meditate – on the love of God.

4. Is it arrogance or is it humility to feel confident in your salvation? Why?

Tune in to the times you're worried about God and how he feels about you. What is going on? What are the triggers that make you question God? What areas of emotional bondage exist for you? When you're at your best does God love you more than he does when you're at your worst? What about right after a big sin, what do you feel about the love of God and the security of your salvation? In what ways do you need a confidence breakthrough?

1. How can we mesh true humility with unshakeable confidence?
2. How do the commonly held views on *repentance* contradict the view offered in this chapter?
3. How does fear keep the faithful faithful? How does it work? How much staying power does this motivation have?
4. How does love keep the faithful faithful? How does it work? How much staying power does this motivation have? What are some key differences?
5. "So that we may boldly say, 'The Lord is my Helper...'" (Hebrews 13:6). Think about the words *boldly* and *my helper*. How is this claim not arrogance?

The Confidence Breakthrough Prayer

Loving Father,

If the death and resurrection of Jesus mean anything, they mean I don't have to fear your presence. You are as satisfied with me as you are with Christ — because you see me as one with him.

I hereby refuse to let *fear* drive my walk with you. Not fear, but love; not worry, but grace fuels me.

I read in your word that I should fear you, and I do — in the sense of honor, respect, and concern for your glory.

But by your grace, and because of Christ, I will not fear punishment from you, disapproval from you, or the removal of your presence or blessing. You wouldn't do those things to Christ, and since, I'm joined to him, you won't do those things to me.

I follow you out of trust, not fear. Out of love, not obligation. With joy, not drudgery. With complete confidence in future grace.

I repent of all beliefs that diminish your compassion and grace. I believe that you are who you say you are, and I am who you say I am.

I approach you with the easy confidence of a firstborn heir. And I say, with all boldness and faith, that I am blessed beyond words to be your child.

In Christ I pray,

Amen.

CHAPTER 9

The Mission Breakthrough

PART 1 — We are Christ's ambassadors, and God is using us to speak to you. We urge you, as though Christ himself were here pleading with you, "Be reconciled to God!" (2 Corinthians 5:20, NLT)

BIG LIE #9

SHARING GOD'S LOVE AND GRACE IN THE WORLD REQUIRES ME TO BE A FREAK.

---

1. In your own words, describe the "Eternal State," the day Jesus Christ "will be seen as reigning King from shore to shore"(pp. 140-141).

2. According to p. 141, why did God leave you on earth after your salvation? What is your response to that? Why might it be a bad idea? Why might it be a glorious idea?

> Your grace mission is the most natural thing in the world once you break through the legalism in your life.

3. Describe righteousness, peace, and joy in terms of grace (p. 142).

PART 2 For you know the grace of our Lord Jesus Christ, that though He was rich, yet for your sakes He became poor, that you through His poverty might become rich. (2 Corinthians 8:9)

Early in *Grace Breakthrough*, you read this verse, and this comment:

> *"If you know Christ, you are, by definition, rich. This verse says so. Which leads to what might be the most common problem among Christians today: Most of God's children limp beneath their true riches in grace." (p. 16)*

1. Describe some breakthroughs, if any, in how you see yourself, God, and life now that you've worked through this book.

2. What does it mean to say that "grace theology needs to become grace psychology"? What are your thoughts about this?

3. Why would having a purpose and mission in life be a natural outflow of grace?

PART 3 1. Fill in this chart of grace-based ways to engage with God's mission.

1	You engage your life mission by…	Thoughts & Reactions
2	You engage your life mission by…	
3	You engage your life mission by…	

PART 4

For the earth will be filled / With the knowledge of the glory of the LORD, / As the waters cover the sea. (Habakkuk 2:14)

1. Page 155 lists several ways in which Jesus invites you to partner in his mission of helping people find and follow God. Which ones resonate with you most? Least? How engaged are you personally in the cause of evangelism and/or world mission?

2. Why is "speaking the words of the gospel of grace" the most important way we engage God's mission? What does Romans 10:14 say about this?

> THERE IS NO SIGN SO GRAND OR WONDER SO GLORIOUS AS A SINFUL SOUL STEPPING ACROSS SALVATION'S THRESHOLD BY GRACE THROUGH FAITH IN THE SAVIOR.

3. Respond to the statement above. How is a person's salvation the greatest miracle of all?

4. How does GRACE lead to a *natural* lifestyle of evangelism?

WEEKEND This weekend, look at the people around you through the lens of grace and salvation. Instead of noticing their faults, notice their needs. Instead of criticizing, try to feel compassion. Instead of wondering about their wealth or appearance, consider whether they know Jesus or not. Pray that God would use you to show his grace to them. That you would move beyond considering your own needs to a place of compassion for the desperate need of salvation for the lost world around you.

DISCUSS 1. What are some ways in which evangelism (outreach to those who don't know Christ) and grace go together?
2. Are you part of a church where lost people are routinely being saved? If you're not part of a church, would you consider attending one? Or...
3. How can individuals help instill the value of evangelism within their churches while still respecting church leadership?
4. How does being your truest, deepest self further the cause of evangelism?
5. How does God's love impel him to be the Great Evangelist (John 3:16)?
6. In what ways is the story of Jesus the greatest love story ever told? The greatest grace ever conceived?

Mission Breakthrough Prayer

Precious Lord,

How I thank you for the people who told me about Jesus and your matchless grace in him. Thank you for those who loved me, prayed for me, answered my questions, taught me, and put up with me while I kicked and fought against grace.

For the Cross of Christ — the fountain of all grace — I give you endless praise. For whatever grace breakthroughs I have made, I give you all the glory. For whatever guilt and shame I have shed at the foot of the Cross, I humbly bless your name.

And now Lord, I want to join the ranks of witnesses who proclaim a grace that still saves the lost. I want my life to be a coming attraction for heaven — a living, breathing proclamation of the matchless grace of Christ.

Equip me, Lord, to lead people to Christ. Use me in the grand adventure of helping lost people receive your great salvation.

I will shine your grace-energized light. I will be my grace-filled self. I will speak the grace-only gospel. I long to tell the old, old story of Jesus and his love. I long to live it too.

And I pray for the day when grace breaks through the hardest hearts I know, to shine the light of the glorious gospel to those who do not believe.

In Christ I pray,

Amen.

CHAPTER 10

Top Ten Grace Breakthroughs

PART 1

But as it is written: "Eye has not seen, nor ear heard, Nor have entered into the heart of man The things which God has prepared for those who love Him." (1 Corinthians 2:9)

BIG LIE #10

NOW THAT I HAVE LEARNED ABOUT GRACE, I CAN MOVE ON TO SOMETHING ELSE.

---

1. When MOSES labeled himself as inadequate to speak to Pharaoh, God promised to "be with his mouth." How would that translate into your own life? In what key areas of your life would you like to hear of God's promised presence?

> NOBODY EVER GRADUATES OUT OF CHRIST'S SCHOOL OF GRACE.

2. JONAH'S breakthrough flopped. He simply refused to soften his heart to the Ninevites' desperate need for grace. Are there areas in your life where you might be resisting God's work to soften your heart?

3. What aspect of grace strikes you most in the story of MEPHIBOSHETH?

PART 2 → 1. How is DAVID'S grace breakthrough an "arrow-reversal maneuver"? How hard is it for most people to have their arrows reversed?

2. NAOMI had a hard time seeing the grace in her life (standing right beside her in the person of Ruth). Dig deep, and make a list of some of the grace-blessings in your life you might often overlook.

3. Have you ever had a problem that "solved itself" like God did for ESTHER? How would you describe that solution as a demonstration of grace?

God can make impossible problems evaporate like the morning fog.

PART 3

> There is therefore now no condemnation to those who are in Christ Jesus, who do not walk according to the flesh, but according to the Spirit. (Romans 8:10)

1. The message Jesus told to the ADULTEROUS WOMAN was important not only for its content but also for its order. Why?

2. Why might we describe the faith of the FOUR LEPERS as a move toward the big, scary thing on the horizon? Why can faith sometimes feel scary?

> **NEVER UNDERESTIMATE THE FALLEN HEART'S ABILITY TO ECLIPSE THE SUNSHINE OF GRACE.**

3. Do you know people who, like the EXODUS GENERATION, prefer the securities of slavery over the risks of liberty? Why might this happen?

PART 4

For it is good that the heart be established by grace...
(Hebrews 13:9)

1. How does PAUL'S grace breakthrough parallel the breakthrough we all need when it comes to truly embracing God's grace?

2. What can make life hard when you are kicking against God's grace-incentives in your life? Are you aware of any ways in which you're resisting grace? What would you like to say to God about them?

3. From the appendix, can you see how storing up God's promises would help stabilize the grace in your heart?

WEEKEND

This weekend, simply enjoy God's grace. Recite his promises. Rest in his love. Revel in your exalted position. Remind yourself of the marvelous, matchless, infinite grace of Almighty God.

DISCUSS

1. What are some other grace breakthroughs in Scripture?
2. What are some grace breakthroughs you've made while working through this book?
3. Share some of your favorite grace-filled Bible verses.
4. When you think about the death of Jesus on the Cross, what do you feel and what big truths come to mind?

Breakthrough Prayer

Gracious Lord,

Break through the scar tissue on my heart. Light up the darkness of my soul. Pierce the hardness, and let your grace break through.

I'm too tired to work any more. I'm too dirty to keep cleaning myself up. I'm too stuck to get unstuck without your help. I'm too little and weak to climb the stairway to heaven. I'm too satisfied, successful, and rich sometimes to even feel my need of you.

So, Lord, take me up by that high and holy elevator of Grace. Let me ride the coattails of my precious Savior all the way to glory.

You have washed away my sin. Now wash away the lies I believe. Heal the festering wounds of Grace Deficit Disorder. And help me rest always and forever in the finished work of Christ, my Savior. Let the Grace Breakthroughs Commence.

In the mighty name of Jesus, and by his matchless grace I pray,

Amen.

BONUS CHAPTER 1

Grace in the Gospels

"For God so loved the world that He gave His only begotten Son, that whoever believes in Him should not perish but have everlasting life." (John 3:16)

Introduction

Grace sets Christianity in a league of its own. In all the religions of all the world for all of time, there's nothing even close to it. It is grace that makes the Christian's heart skip a beat. It is grace that makes the unbelieving heart object. It is grace that signals the end of legalism, the end of religiosity, the end of self-righteousness, the end of ritualism, the end of self-promoting arrogance, the end of human effort as a means to God. The Bible teaches amazing grace. The Church has sung its sweet sound for centuries.

Yet it is so easy to lose the amazement, and it is so easy to forget the grace. Even worse, there are passages in the Bible that, on first reading, seem to contradict grace altogether. These passages make us question grace. They make us doubt our grace breakthroughs.

You'll find many of the difficult Scriptures concentrated in certain places in the Bible, like the Old Testament and, surprisingly, the gospels (the books that tell the story of Jesus: Matthew, Mark, Luke, and John). Some Bible experts suggest that these books are not "grace-books" because they belong to "an age of law" when God worked in different ways.

May I lovingly disagree.

Grace flavors every part of Scripture as salt flavors the sea. Actually, grace isn't just the salt. It's the whole sea.

But it looks funny in different parts of Scripture, especially gospels. It isn't straightforward, in-your-face, logically-argued grace like it is in the teaching portions of Scripture. Instead, in the gospels, grace appears in stories and, especially, in the order in which they're told. Grace is easy to miss. It's subtle.

Jesus knew this would happen. He actually thanked God for the confusion. He said that the teachings of grace in the gospels can only be unlocked by a person whose heart is in the right place:

> At that time Jesus answered and said, "I thank You, Father, Lord of heaven and earth, that You have hidden these things from the wise and prudent and have revealed them to babes." (Matthew 11:25)

Why is grace so hard to find in the gospels?

Because it is hidden from those who will not take their rightful place in the lineup of the world's charity cases.

So let's check our pride at the door. I'd like to look at one of the more difficult chapters in the gospels to interpret in light of grace. It's loaded with seemingly anti-grace sentiment. My goal is to quiet the doubts about grace that the Enemy loves to stir up in your mind.

It's the Sequence

Back in the pre-computer days, when dinosaurs roamed the earth, teachers taught their students to use index cards to prepare essays. We would jot down key ideas and relevant notes, one main idea per card. If we were writing a very long essay, we would produce a thick stack of index cards, each with scribbles, and quotes, and data and sources. Then we would arrange the cards in order, make some adjustments, omit some, use some, and write our essays.

Think of the gospel authors—Matthew, Mark (some say with Peter's help), Luke, and John—as essayists. Each one had a stack of ancient index cards. Each card held a story, a parable, a teaching, or an episode from the life of Jesus.

Each gospel writer arranged the index cards and wrote his gospel. But they wrote them with slight [insignificant] differences. They included some index cards and omitted others. They rearranged them. They shuffled the order sometimes.

They edited, the stories, but not in a bad way.

Why? Were they confused? Inaccurate? Did they get their facts wrong? Were they being sneaky?

No, not at all.

Each gospel author laid his index cards in a certain *sequence* in order to make theological points. They were less interested in chronology—though that is an important part—and more interested in theology. The sequence mattered as much as the stories themselves. The sequence and structure are, therefore, an essential part of interpretation. This is how they wrote theology back then.

And the beautiful thing is that the theology of each gospel writer—Matthew, Mark, Luke, and John—meshes perfectly with the theology of each other gospel writer, and with all of the other writers of Scripture too.

It's the sequence (context) that helps each author make his point. In fact, if you just take one index card out of the stack, and isolate it from its neighbors, you'll miss the point. You might get it wrong. You might even reverse the point and get it exactly backwards.

You might make grace sound very ungracious.

All of which is to say that the Scriptures, and especially the gospels, can only be interpreted in light of their context. It is by these sequences and structures, all of them inspired by the Holy Spirit, that the Scripture authors make their points.

Especially in the gospels.

And it is by missing these sequences that interpreters overlook the grace that has been staring them in the face all along.

Case in point, Mark 10.

Let's dig for diamonds.

BONUS CHAPTER 2

Grace in the Gospels, part 2

Section 1: The Need for Grace
The Pharisees, Disciples and Divorce, vv. 1-12

Then He arose from there and came to the region of Judea by the other side of the Jordan. And multitudes gathered to Him again, and as He was accustomed, He taught them again. The Pharisees came and asked Him, "Is it lawful for a man to divorce his wife?" testing Him. And He answered and said to them, "What did Moses command you?" They said, "Moses permitted a man to write a certificate of divorce, and to dismiss her." And Jesus answered and said to them, "Because of the hardness of your heart he wrote you this precept. But from the beginning of the creation, God 'made them male and female.' 'For this reason a man shall leave his father and mother and be joined to his wife, 'and the two shall become one flesh'; so then they are no longer two, but one flesh. Therefore what God has joined together, let not man separate." In the house His disciples also asked Him again about the same matter. So He said to them, "Whoever divorces his wife and marries another commits adultery against her. And if a woman divorces her husband and marries another, she commits adultery." (Mark 10:1-12)

Throngs of people crowded around Jesus. In this paragraph, the Pharisees asked him a question. These were highly religious people. But their religion was very rule oriented. The scribes and Pharisees were custodians of countless rules and regulations. The Pharisees prided themselves on unflinching obedience to God's laws. Here they ask Jesus a question.

"Is it lawful...?" they say.

Christ answers with a question: "What does Moses say?" The Pharisees correctly point out that Moses, the law-giver, permitted divorce under the condition of adultery. That's in Deuteronomy 24:1, a book Moses wrote roughly 1,500 years before Christ.

But then Christ took the topic of divorce to a deeper level. Not only did Moses write Deuteronomy 24:1, which permitted divorce in the case of adultery, he also wrote Genesis 2:24, which stated that a man and woman become one flesh when they get married. God joins them together, and therefore humans should not tear them apart. It is on this premise that Jesus teaches his disciples (vv. 10-12) that divorce and remarriage is always a form of something called adultery. This should make us all squirm a bit.

By now you ought to be scratching your head asking, "Where's the grace?" Simply this: the Law of God permits divorce, but only as a concession to human sin and weakness. Or as Jesus put it, "because of the hardness of your heart" (v. 5). God permits divorce, but God never likes divorce (does anybody?), and all divorce is ultimately a violation of the original principle of marriage. The original principle of marriage is one man, one woman, one flesh, one lifetime.

So what?

Christ's point is that you can be technically very good at following God's rules, but that still doesn't make you righteous.

You can be very correct in your behavior (i.e., never divorced, or only divorced "for the right reasons"), and very far from God in your heart.

So Jesus looks around the circle at these very correct people. The best of the best. Righteous people. They obeyed all God's laws in behavior, but still missed God's heart by a mile. Some had been legally divorced. All had lusted. All had committed adultery, whether physically or mentally. Yet they considered themselves tight with God.

So tight, in fact, that they didn't need grace in order to reach him. Knowing the danger of this self-delusion, Jesus said something shocking.

So Jesus looked around the circle, made eye contact with each Pharisee one by one, and in effect said, "You're a sinner. You're a sinner. You're a sinner. You're a sinner. And you're a sinner, too."

Because even if you think you're doing everything "lawfully," in the eyes of God, you're still a mess. And that is exactly what the Pharisees needed to hear, what the disciples needed to hear, and even what we need to hear.

Do not think that you will get to heaven by keeping rules and regulations. Do not think that you will impress God or even please God by external conformity to his law. Even when you keep the Bible's rules and regulations, you still fall short. You are imperfect, and always will be imperfect. Every member of the human race has sinned. Every one of us is the moral equivalent of an adulterer. Don't set yourself on some pedestal, point to a few rules you've kept—even the biblical rules—and think that God is impressed. God never blesses defective human righteousness, no matter how sincere or even "lawful."

How many misguided interpreters have combed through this passage for picky little rules about adultery and divorce! We're going to see it's not about that at all. It's about something else altogether. But that's the unavoidable mistake you make when you rip Scripture out of its sequence.

The first index card Mark included in his chapter ten stack teaches the difficult news that every one of us, no matter how good we are, stands in need of the grace of God. It's a prelude to grace. It establishes our need. No one is ever so successful, decent, brave, or clean that they rise above their desperate need for grace. That's lesson one—less about adultery and all about the universal human need for grace. Get it?

Here's lesson two.

Section 2: The Attitude of Grace
Jesus and the Children, vv. 13-16

Then they brought little children to Him, that He might touch them; but the disciples rebuked those who brought them. But when Jesus saw it, He was greatly displeased and said to them, "Let the little children come to Me, and do not forbid them; for of such is the kingdom of God. Assuredly, I say to you, whoever does not receive the kingdom of God as a little child will by no means enter it." And He took them up in His arms, put His hands on them, and blessed them. (Mark 10:13-16)

When we in Western Civilization think of children, it's likely that warm, fuzzy, affectionate feelings come to mind. Children are precious. Innocent. We value them.

Not so in much of the ancient world. Children were not precious, not valued, and not endearing. The original readers of Mark's gospel would have very little of the feelings of affection that we have today. Children were viewed as property, like livestock on a farm. They were routinely discarded. At best, people felt that children should be seen and not heard. The disciples display this disdain for children when they rebuke parents for bringing some children to Jesus. They exercised the spiritual gift of being bouncers.

"Get those nasty little kids away from Jesus!"

That's why, in the gospels, children frequently represent a category of people that we could call Life's Last in Line. They are routinely lumped together with lepers, tax collectors, prostitutes, poor people, and the like. People who are morally last in line. What does Jesus say about people who are last in the moral line up of the universe?

> "Permit the little children to come to me, and forbid them not, for such is the kingdom of God. Truly I say to you, whoever shall not receive the kingdom of God as a little child shall not enter in."

The only people who qualify for God's grace are people who put themselves in the category of life's last in line.

Without this humble attitude, grace will sail past you like a cloud in a windy sky.

In the first section, the Pharisees, and even the disciples, wanted to pat themselves on the back for being first in line. Moral. Decent. Religious. Thrifty. Righteous. Lawful.

So here, in the second paragraph, Jesus blew them all away. "Fine," he said. "Pretend you're first in line. But realize that you'll be totally disqualified for grace." You only qualify for the grace of God when you see yourself morally as one of life's big losers.

"Amazing grace, how sweet the sound that saved" a what?

"A wretch like me."

The children in this passage do not represent innocence; they represent unworthiness. (I'm not saying I agree with that assessment; it's just how the people of the day thought.) That's what would have come to mind for Mark's original readers, and that's what should come to mind for us when we interpret it.

Not big in the eyes of God, little.

Not worthy, but unworthy.

These are the ones who Jesus wraps up in his arms and blesses.

Mark laid his index cards in a perfect grace-sequence when he wrote this chapter. The first card he picked showed the need for grace—no matter how good you are, you still fall short. The second card showed the required attitude for grace—I am humble enough to admit my unworthiness and to declare my need of a Savior.

Here's the third card.

Section 3: The Antithesis of Grace
The Rich Young Ruler, vv. 17-22

> Now as He was going out on the road, one came running, knelt before Him, and asked Him, "Good Teacher, what shall I do that I may inherit eternal life?" So Jesus said to him, "Why do you call Me good? No one is good but One, that is, God. You know the commandments: 'Do not commit adultery,' 'Do not murder,' 'Do not steal,' 'Do not bear false witness,' 'Do not defraud,' 'Honor your father and your mother.'" And he answered and said to Him, "Teacher, all these things I have kept from my youth." Then Jesus, looking at him, loved him, and said to him, "One thing you lack: Go your way, sell whatever you have and give to the poor, and you will have treasure in heaven; and come, take up the cross, and follow Me." But he was sad at this word, and went away sorrowful, for he had great possessions. (Mark 10:17-22)

This section has been misused as a weapon to bludgeon the grace right out of the gospel.

See, if you want eternal life, keep his commandments.

See, sell your goods, sacrifice your self, and you can have eternal life.

See, take up your cross and follow Jesus, or no eternal life for you!

No grace to see here. Move along. Get busy for God, or else!

Ouch.

Is Jesus really teaching that we get to heaven by keeping the commandments? Not one bit. He merely answers the young man in terms of the young man's question.

The question is, "What shall I do that I may inherit eternal life?" Emphasize the word "do." What shall I perform? What effort shall I put forth? What merit badges must I earn?

So Jesus tells him to keep the Ten Commandments and all the other laws.

A performance-based question merits a performance-based answer.

Jesus knew his heart and was pushing him to a realization about it.

I don't know how this guy can keep a straight face when he replies, "All these laws I have kept from the time I was a youth." It's as if he said, "Jesus, no problem. When it comes to the Ten Commandments, I'm batting a thousand."

I would have said, "Let me ask your mother."

But notice Jesus' reply. "Okay. If you're going to ride this train, ride it all the way to the end. Sell all your stuff, give it away, take a vow of poverty, take up the cross, and follow me."

What does that mean? Is that really the gospel of our salvation?

No. It means that if you're going to obtain heaven or God's grace or God's blessing or spiritual maturity, or any good gift from God whatsoever, on the basis of your works, then you have to go with your works all the way.

You have to earn every merit badge in the manual.

You have to be totally, one hundred percent perfect, one hundred percent moral, decent, thrifty, brave, and clean, all the time.

If you're going to board the train of performance, you have to ride it to the end.

And the end, if you're honest, is failure, which is the perfect set up for grace.

Like the Pharisees, this man put himself at the front of the line, and Jesus was lovingly trying to shove him to the back of the line where he belonged. But it didn't work, and the man went away sad.

Stubborn mule.

This is the opposite of the desired outcome. The message Jesus preached here was not the gospel, and was not grace, and was not intended to be either. This man couldn't hear of grace because he was too busy shouting his own excellence.

He wasn't open to any message in which Someone Else had to pay his freight to heaven.

And when Jesus laid the total cost on him, the man knew he couldn't pay the freight himself.

But he was too proud to say so.

So he went away sad.

It is an enormous mistake to interpret these words as part of the gospel, or as instructions for the way of salvation. They do not offer up grace at all. They only tee up the ball up for grace. They're a prelude.

In context, they are a way of shoving one man's nose in his own imperfections—a man who refused to acknowledge them.

This isn't grace.

It's the antithesis of grace.

The antithesis of grace is claiming you qualify for heaven because you keep God's laws. That's Mark's third index card.

Section 4: The Origin of Grace
The Eye of the Needle, vv. 23-27

Then Jesus looked around and said to His disciples, "How hard it is for those who have riches to enter the kingdom of God!" And the disciples were astonished at His words. But Jesus answered again and said to them, "Children, how hard it is for those who trust in riches to enter the kingdom of God! It is easier for a camel to go through the eye of a needle than for a rich man to enter the kingdom of God." And they were greatly astonished, saying among themselves, "Who then can be saved?" But Jesus looked at them and said, "With men it is impossible, but not with God; for with God all things are possible." (Mark 10:23-27)

Here we have the famous saying about a camel going through the eye of a needle.

The disciples ask, "Who then can be saved?" This question is parallel with the rich young ruler's question, "What shall I do to inherit eternal life" (v. 17)? Which is also parallel with Jesus statement about "entering the kingdom of God" (v. 15). Which is also parallel with the Pharisees question in v. 2, "Is it lawful." In other words, each section of this chapter asks one all-important question: *How can I be properly connected with God for time and eternity?* So far, each answer has been the same: *not by your own efforts or morality, but only by the efforts of God.*

The same is true of this paragraph. The key question is, "Who than can be saved? inherit eternal life? enter the kingdom of heaven? be considered lawful before God?"

Jesus says, "With men this is impossible." Or, we could translate it this way, "this is humanly impossible." Let that sink into your brain. This is humanly impossible. It's not hard; it's utterly, absolutely, eternally impossible.

Apart from a miraculous work of divine grace, you and I have zero chance of entering the kingdom of heaven. Labor all you want. Give all you can. Sacrifice, sweat, and strain. Do everything possible and it still won't be enough.

"It's harder for a camel to go through the eye of a needle than for a rich man to enter the kingdom of heaven." The picture is ludicrous on purpose. So is salvation by self-effort.

Sadly, most people still clutch their moral bankbooks and think they'll buy their way in.

I can imagine Jesus looking his disciples in the eye and asking, "Just what part of *impossible* do you not understand?"

After blasting away the impossibility of an earned salvation, Jesus offers hope. What is humanly impossible is always divinely possible. "But not with God; for with God all things are possible." The Greek word translated possible is *dunamis*. *Dunamis* means power. When you dig through all the layers of grace and get to bedrock, you'll find, a) the omnipotence of God and, b) the inability of humans.

Until you take your place with the rest of us "poor in spirit" slobs, there's no heaven for you. That's the starting point, the origin of all grace teaching.

What we can't do, God can do: forgive your sins, heal your broken heart, supply your need, restore your brokenness, slather you with grace to last forever.

In each section someone is clinging to some kind of human ability: 1) the Pharisees to their morality; 2) the disciples to their adult superiority; 3) the young ruler to his law-keeping; 4) the rich to their riches. All of these people think that human ability will put them at the front of God's line. Well it won't, because the origin of grace is always in the ability of God.

Mark's index cards have been laid in perfect order.

Enter Peter with yet another bonehead challenge to grace.

Bonus Chapter 3

Grace in the Gospels, part 3

Section 5: The Cost-Benefit Analysis of Grace
We Have Left All, vv. 28-31

> Then Peter began to say to Him, "See, we have left all and followed You." So Jesus answered and said, "Assuredly, I say to you, there is no one who has left house or brothers or sisters or father or mother or wife or children or lands, for My sake and the gospel's, who shall not receive a hundredfold now in this time—houses and brothers and sisters and mothers and children and lands, with persecutions—and in the age to come, eternal life. But many who are first will be last, and the last first." (Mark 10:28-31)

This is yet another paragraph where it's easy to miss the point about grace. Again, as in every other paragraph so far, someone is making a moral claim on God. This time it's Peter. He says, "Jesus notice this. Notice my good works. We have left all and followed you."

Now isn't this a good thing? No. Not in this context and not with Peter's attitude. Peter focuses on the price he himself has paid, not on the price Christ is about to pay.

We have left all and followed you. Yet another approach to Jesus based on performance. Do you see the pattern? Do you see Mark's arrangement?

I love Peter, because he makes me feel better about the many times I've been an idiot too.

How does Jesus respond?

Gently.

Jesus could have slammed Peter. "You think you've left all? You think you've given stuff up? You actually have the nerve to look *me* in the face and talk about the price you have paid? Are you that blind?"

But Jesus was gentle.

He acknowledged that some indeed do pay a price when they embrace Jesus and his gospel. But that price is not really a price. It has no redemptive value. No saving worth. No monetary value in heaven's realm. It's tough in a lot of cultures. People may hate you. You may lose property or wealth or status or friends. Your own family may reject you when they find out.

Jesus acknowledged that reality. He understood that Peter turned his back on a lucrative business to follow him. Jesus did not pretend that didn't happen.

However, what Peter has given up will be so abundantly repaid in this life and the life to come, his so-called sacrifice really doesn't amount to anything.

Jesus basically says, "By comparison to the riches of heaven, by comparison to what you gain, and by comparison to what I left to come to you, you, Peter, have given up nothing."

On the gigantic radar screen of grace, whatever you may give up to embrace Jesus isn't even a blip.

In chapter ten, Mark assembles story after story of people approaching Jesus on their own worthiness, and bouncing off of him like bullets off Superman's chest.

Anyone who makes "leaving homes and loved ones" the cost of salvation based on this paragraph of Scripture has mastered the art of missing the point.

Christ crucified is the cost of your salvation.

Anything else fades into oblivion.

It's at this point that Jesus serves up his classic, head-scratching, line: "For many that are first shall be last, and the last shall be first."

What if Jesus asked the human race to line up in order of goodness? Or morality? Or moral worth?

Where would you put yourself in that line? Toward the front, with the moral winners, or toward the back, with the moral losers?

Think hard.

The first will be... well, you get the point. Grace is counterintuitive. It's the opposite of what the unrenewed fringes of your mind still think.

In the great, cosmic, cost-benefit analysis, Christ pays everything, you gain everything, and whatever you think you have paid amounts to nothing.

Welcome to a massive grace breakthrough.

Section 6: The True Cost of Grace
Jesus Predicts His Death & Resurrection, vv. 32-34

> Now they were on the road, going up to Jerusalem, and Jesus was going before them; and they were amazed. And as they followed they were afraid. Then He took the twelve aside again and began to tell them the things that would happen to Him: "Behold, we are going up to Jerusalem, and the Son of Man will be betrayed to the chief priests and to the scribes; and they will condemn Him to death and deliver Him to the Gentiles; and they will mock Him, and scourge Him, and spit on Him, and kill Him. And the third day He will rise again." (Mark 10:32-34)

In this paragraph Mark turns a corner. Up to now, each event was triggered by a question or claim in which someone claimed moral superiority. But in this paragraph, the action and words all belong to Jesus.

Mark tells us the disciples were dazed and afraid. They were so confused that they didn't know which end was up. Why? Because when the grace of God begins to penetrate your thick legalistic hide, the first thing you feel is confused and afraid.

Grace breakthroughs can be scary.

You'll be okay.

Don't miss the order of Mark's line up. As they head toward Jerusalem, Jesus is in front of the line. Mark makes a point of this. He writes, "Jesus went before them (v. 32), and they followed."

Think about it.

Now who's last in line? Nice touch, Mark.

When grace breaks through, you recognize that only Jesus has a claim to be first in the moral lineup, and you always belong at the end.

That is Mark's setup for this short speech of Jesus.

That speech is all about his work, his effort, and the price he pays. He will be condemned to death. His death will be the responsibility of both Jews and Gentiles—in other words, of the whole human race. He will be humiliated, mocked, whipped, spit upon, and killed. Though Jesus focuses on his upcoming death, he also reveals that death does not win in the end. He will rise again.

Whenever Jesus predicts his own death, Bible scholars call that a "Passion Prediction." This is based on the Latin word for suffering, *passio*. This is the third Passion Prediction in Mark (8:31; 9:31). After just about every Passion Prediction, the disciples of Jesus do or say something stupid. We'll see that in the next paragraph.

Why does Mark place a Passion Prediction here in this sequence of paragraphs?

As these paragraphs have marched across the page like soldiers in formation, Mark has shown over and over that whatever price has to be paid to get you into heaven cannot be paid by you. Not your religious, legal obedience (the Pharisees). Not your superiority (the disciples). Not your keeping God's laws (the rich young ruler). Not your power (the wealthy). Not even your devotion to Christ (Peter and the disciples).

It's just not you.

So then, what is the price of your salvation? The blood of Christ. The price of your salvation is entirely paid by Christ in his death and resurrection.

All of it.

Paid in full.

Do you realize what this means? You can go to heaven, you can be legally acceptable to God, you can be a citizen of the kingdom of God, you can be saved... if and only if you admit you are a sinner in need of a Savior, and turn to Jesus in faith alone for salvation by grace alone.

No merit badges required. No human goodness in view. No efforts. No rituals. No claim on God, except what Christ has done on the cross.

After 31 verses of legalism, the spotlight in this chapter shines finally on the work of Christ. That's what grace is all about. Grace is about God doing for you what you could never do for yourself. Grace is what we preach because grace is what Scripture teaches, and grace is what Christ purchased.

Let's tune our hearts to the verbs that Jesus uses in his Passion Prediction. He uses eight of them.

1. *Will be betrayed.* The Greek word (*paradidomi*) means to deliver up treacherously. This verb is spelled a certain way that makes it a passive voice, which simply means that Jesus will allow himself to be betrayed by others. It's amazing to think that the Lord of glory would permit himself to be betrayed. He didn't have to do it, but that's how much Jesus loved you.
2. *They will condemn.* The Greek word (*katakrino*) means to judge guilty of a crime worthy of punishment. Though he was sinless and guiltless, they condemned him. The Bible teaches that Jesus was condemned for sins he did not commit. Only this gospel of grace deals with the human condition, not by creating a fiction and pretending we hadn't sinned. And not by violating divine holiness and pretending God could overlook our sins. Only this gospel of grace deals fully with our sins by condemning every last one of them in Jesus Christ on the old, rugged cross, on a hill called Mt. Calvary.
3. *Deliver him to the Gentiles.* Same verb as *betrayed.* Jesus was betrayed first to the Jewish leaders, and then to Gentile powers. Why mention both? Because the whole human race is guilty of the death of Jesus.
4. *Mock him.* This verb is particularly gruesome. It is the verb *empaizo. Paizo* means to play, to toy with something. The prefix

em- is an intensifier. The crucifiers of Jesus will toy with him first. The Bible says they mockingly called him King of the Jews. They put a scepter in his hands, and hammered a crown of thorns into his head. They blindfolded him, and punched him, and asked who hit him. They bowed to him as they beat him with sticks. It's too easy to forget what the Cross of Christ really meant. It's easy to sanitize it. Analyze it. Sentimentalize it. Take it for granted. The Cross was the most gruesome spectacle ever staged in human history. Never forget the price Jesus paid to save your soul.

5. *Spit on him.* The Bible connects spitting with ultimate shame, ultimate embarrassment, ultimate rejection (cf., Job 30:10, Deut. 25:9, Isa. 50:6). This is as humiliating as it can get. What is so amazing is that Jesus could have stopped it at any time. With a word from his mouth, he could have caused his tormentors to die. But he took it all so we could be saved. That is amazing, and that is grace.

6. *Scourge him.* The Roman scourge was a kind of whip. It was an instrument of torture. The tails of the whip were embedded with bits of glass and metal. When a convict was scourged, his back, sides, and chest were shredded down to the bone. It's far easier to make a pretty cross out of silver and gold, and to dangle it on a chain around your neck, than to look at the bare facts of the crucifixion of Jesus. There he was, bloodied, but unbowed. Giving his back, his head, his hands, his feet, his all, that we might live forever. All our puny efforts fade to nothingness in light of the horrible splendor of the Cross.

7. *Kill him.* Two short words. Kill him. Jesus knew he was going to suffer. He knew he was going to be nailed to the Cross. Thick spikes driven through hands and feet. Stood up, hanging between heaven and earth. Nailed to the Cross. What horror! He knew he was going to die. The death of Jesus Christ was the most agonizing death any human has ever suffered. Not only because of the horrendous physical suffering, but because of

the even more horrendous spiritual suffering he endured. More painful than the nails, and the scourge, more humiliating than the spitting and the mocking, more heartbreaking than the betrayal, the worst pain that Jesus felt was the pain when our sins hit him. God laid on him the sins of us all, and God executed Christ for those sins. That is the price of our salvation. That is the only price. It is the only conceivable price. It is such an all-sufficient price that it insults God to even try to throw coins into the mix as if Jesus had not done enough. That is why Jesus died, and that was the worst part of it all. But thank God, death did not win the day.

8. *Rise again.* This is the bright spot in the whole Passion Prediction. He will conquer sin. He will put death to death. He will defeat Satan and embarrass the demons. He will purchase forgiveness full and free. He will burst open the gates of hell, and shred the bars of death. Christ will rise again. Christ wins. Christ conquers. Christ over all! This is the only good news worth calling good news. And it is all accomplished by Jesus and only by Jesus. Not one speck of human effort can intrude on this perfect work of Christ. It is a finished work, a perfect work, an all-sufficient work, and an exclusive work. Nothing we do counts. It's all Jesus, and all Jesus alone.

Mark has just devastated legalism. He has shown over and over that whatever price has to be paid to get you into heaven cannot be paid by you. Not your religious obedience. Not your maturity. Not your morality. Not your law keeping. Not your money. Not your power. Not you.

What will it take to get this through our heads and into our hearts?

What is the price of your salvation? The price of your salvation is the blood of Christ. The price has been entirely paid by Jesus Christ in his death and resurrection. All of it. Paid in full. Finished.

What is the price of your salvation? More than you can ever pay.

That is why salvation must be received as a gift, on the basis of grace, or else you cannot receive it at all. Imagine yourself walking up to God in heaven. There sits Jesus at his right hand. He still bears the scars in his hands and feet from the nails. He still has the scars on his head from the thorns. He still has the scar in his side from the spear. That is the price he paid.

Then, imagine yourself walking up to God waving the moral equivalent of a fifty-dollar bill, and saying, "Excuse me, God, but are you good with this?" If fifty dollars doesn't seem enough, make it the biggest number you can imagine. No difference.

Was Christ's death not enough? Can you improve on what he did?

Mark beats the drum that you have nothing to give that can possibly obtain heaven for you. You are morally broke, spiritually bankrupt, ethically disabled. Therefore, whatever price had to be paid to get you into heaven was paid in full by Jesus Christ. So quit trying to pay a price that's already been paid.

The true cost of discipleship is the shed blood of Jesus on the Cross, and nothing else matters.

Listen to the Word of God. Quit listening to legalistic preachers. Quit listening to those who undermine your confidence in Christ. Quit paying attention to books, and web sites, and articles, and conferences that make you feel guilty, and cast the burden of salvation onto your puny shoulders. Quit reopening the scabs of legalism. Settle into Christ, and don't let any Pharisee disturb your rest. Cease the endless debates. Quit feeling good about your doubts.

Look at the Cross, choose grace, and don't turn back.

Look to Christ, and don't look back.

He is enough. He is more than enough. He is all you need. Respect him. Respect his sacrifice for you.

Trust in the Passion of the Christ. Cling to the Cross. Cherish the Old, Rugged Cross.

And believe that every grace, every blessing, every treasure God has to give you for time and eternity is paid for in that Cross forever.

This is what Jesus is telling you. This is what Jesus told his disciples. Did they really get it yet?

Unfortunately, no.

Section 7: Blindness to Grace
The Greatness of the Disciples. vv. 35-45

Then James and John, the sons of Zebedee, came to Him, saying, "Teacher, we want You to do for us whatever we ask." And He said to them, "What do you want Me to do for you?" They said to Him, "Grant us that we may sit, one on Your right hand and the other on Your left, in Your glory." But Jesus said to them, "You do not know what you ask. Are you able to drink the cup that I drink, and be baptized with the baptism that I am baptized with?" They said to Him, "We are able." So Jesus said to them, "You will indeed drink the cup that I drink, and with the baptism I am baptized with you will be baptized; but to sit on My right hand and on My left is not Mine to give, but it is for those for whom it is prepared." And when the ten heard it, they began to be greatly displeased with James and John. But Jesus called them to Himself and said to them, "You know that those who are considered rulers over the Gentiles lord it over them, and their great ones exercise authority over them. Yet it shall not be so among you; but whoever desires to become great among you shall be your servant. And whoever of you desires to be first shall be slave of all. For even the Son of Man did not come to be served, but to serve, and to give His life a ransom for many." (Mark 10:35-45)

I told you that whenever Jesus predicted his death, his disciples did something stupid.

Jesus predicts his horrible death, and his best friends get in a tug of war over who gets the best seats at heaven's banquet table.

Nice friends.

James and John start it. They approach Jesus secretly, asking for seats of honor in heaven. When the other disciples find out, they're angry, only because James and John beat them to it.

Apparently the "first shall be last" lesson didn't stick.

No matter how hard Jesus tries to teach grace, it just doesn't sink in. We've already seen that the human heart is terminally resistant to grace. Let's call the disciples Exhibit A.

You can probably call me Exhibit B.

Don't look smug—you're probably Exhibit C.

When James and John approach Jesus, he asks, "What do you want me to do for you?" Like every other paragraph in this chapter, somebody approaches Jesus with a want, a desire, or a request.

These extremely humble brothers ask to sit at the right and left hand of Jesus, thus occupying forever positions of glory and honor.

Way to think ahead, guys!

Jesus responds with a statement and a question.

The statement is "you do not know what you ask for." Which is a nice way of telling them they're clueless.

To obtain the same glory Jesus has would require paying the same price Jesus pays. Are you guys up for that?

"You bet!" they say. "We can drink the cup that you drink, and be baptized with the baptism that you'll be baptized with. Count us in, one hundred and ten percent!"

I don't think they understood that the cup was a cup of suffering and the baptism was a baptism of death.

Jesus says, "Are you worthy? Can you pay the price that I'm about to pay?"

"Totally worthy and totally able," they say.

Near-terminal hyper-immunity to grace.

Should we laugh or cry?

Yes, they will suffer, they will hurt, they will be persecuted for their faith (that's what Christ's prophecy of v. 39 means). But, in no way is their suffering and persecution even a tiny bit comparable to the suffering and death of Jesus. Plus, it has no redemptive value at all.

By claiming to deserve heavenly glory, the disciples stupidly join the ranks of the Pharisees and the rich young rulers of the world. They make a claim on God based on their own ability, their own morality, their own goodness... the direct opposite of grace.

Even the best of Christ's followers can be dull. We're prone to legalism. That's why we need constant reminders of grace. By your own record, you do not deserve a seat in heaven, much less the seat of honor. All of the honor goes to Christ alone. The rest of us are dragged in on his coattails.

But nobody in this chapter seems to get it.

Until you come to the very end.

Mark has saved the best for last.

In this case, it's true: the last shall be first.

Section 8: The Example of Grace
Blind Bartimaeus. vv. 46-52

> Now they came to Jericho. As He went out of Jericho with His disciples and a great multitude, blind Bartimaeus, the son of Timaeus, sat by the road begging. And when he heard that it was Jesus of Nazareth, he began to cry out and say, "Jesus, Son of David, have mercy on me!" Then many warned him to be quiet; but he cried out all the more, "Son of David, have mercy on me!" So Jesus stood still and commanded him to be called. Then they called the blind man, saying to him, "Be of good cheer. Rise, He is calling you." And throwing aside his garment, he rose and came to Jesus. So Jesus answered and said to him, "What do you want Me to do for you?" The blind man said to Him, "Rabboni, that I may receive my sight." Then Jesus said to him, "Go your way; your faith has made you well." And immediately he received his sight and followed Jesus on the road. (Mark 10:46-52)

The way Mark constructed this chapter is absolutely brilliant. Nobody gets grace. So now it's time to meet Blind Bartimaeus, the unlikely hero of our story. He follows a long line of come-to-Jesus failures:

- Section 1, the Pharisees don't get it.
- Section 2, the disciples don't get it.
- Section 3, the rich young ruler doesn't get it.
- Section 4, the world's winners don't get it.

- Section 5, again, the disciples don't get it. Nobody gets grace. So...
- Section 6, Jesus describes his death as the true cost of grace. Now, somebody should get it, right? Well, in...
- Section 7, the disciples still don't get it.

Finally, here in section 8, Mark introduces us to dear, messed up, pathetic, bankrupt, Blind Bartimaeus. HE GETS IT.

Hallelujah!

He is the example of grace. His approach to Jesus is the one to model. Step into his shoes. Be like him. Receive grace like he did.

Mark makes Blind Bartimaeus the poster child for grace.

Let's notice how Mark describes his condition. He is blind. Not only does Mark use the word "blind" to *describe* him, he uses the word blind to *name* him. Blind has become part of his identity.

He's not only blind but bankrupt, too. The text says he sat by the road begging. No money. No job.

This man is basically helpless, hopeless, bankrupt, and pitiable. He has nothing to offer God. He has no way to pay for his deliverance. In a theological sense that is true for every last one of us. We may not be blind and poor in the physical realm, but because we are sinners, we are all blind and bankrupt in the spiritual realm.

Until you can put yourself in the shoes of Blind Bartimaeus, you cannot cry out from the heart the words that won the day with Jesus. What was that cry from his heart?

"Have mercy on me!"

Think about that.

That is the polar opposite of every other person in this chapter who approaches Jesus.

Does he appeal to God on the basis of what he deserves? What he has earned? How good he is? How moral he is? How religious he is? How baptized, confirmed, communed, and confessed he is?

No. None of this.

He doesn't say, "Pay me what I've earned."

He says, "Have mercy on me!" Give me goodness I haven't earned.

How unlike the Pharisees and the disciples and the wealthy, and the rich young ruler! They all asked God for what they deserved, but Blind Bartimaeus asked for *mercy*. In the Bible the words *mercy* and *grace* are almost synonyms. Both refer to kind and loving gifts from God. *Grace* emphasizes kind and loving gifts for those who don't deserve it. *Mercy* emphasizes kind and loving gifts for those who are pathetic and wretched and miserable. Both words presuppose that the person who receives the kind and loving gifts has no claim on God.

No matter how many people tell Blind Bartimaeus to shut up, he just keeps yelling for mercy (vv. 48,9).

If you feel at all like Bartimaeus—lost, helpless and hopeless—Mark tells you to ignore every voice that is telling you to give up. Reach out for God's mercy no matter who tries to turn you away.

When Bartimaeus came to Jesus, Mark tells us he threw aside his garment and ran to Jesus.

This man had nothing. And now he comes to Jesus with less than nothing. No claims. No pretense. No goodness or righteousness of his own.

There's an old couplet that says, "Nothing in my hands I bring, / Simply to Thy Cross I cling."

There's your grace.

Jesus asks Bartimaeus the same question he asked his disciples (v. 36). "What do you want me to do for you?"

In fact, this question really defines the whole chapter. There are two, and only two, possible answers: A) I want you to save me because I deserve it and I'm so worthy; or B) I want you to save me even though I don't deserve it and am entirely unworthy.

In every preceding paragraph, people offer Answer A to Jesus. They've been stuck on the wrong side of a breakthrough. But now, Jesus asks again, and this time, finally, for the first time in fifty-one long verses, somebody gets it right. And that somebody is one of life's big losers, one of life's outcasts, one of life's last in line.

Finally, somebody offers Answer B: Lord, have mercy on me. I want you to save me even though I don't deserve it and am entirely unworthy. Please save a wretch like me.

In saving him, Jesus highlights the central point of this chapter. "Your *faith* has made you well."

Salvation by grace through faith is the golden thread linking together every page of Scripture.

Not observing the rules and regulations of the Pharisees.

Not being mature or superior like the disciples.

Not keeping the Ten Commandments, or selling your possessions, or giving to the poor, or following Jesus like the rich young ruler.

Not giving up everything for Jesus like the disciples.

Not claiming to be worthy like James and John.

Nothing you do, nothing you perform, nothing you observe can wash your sins away. Just enough faith to trust in Jesus and his death as your only hope, and to say, "Lord, have mercy on broken-down me."

If you're thinking, "That's it? That's too easy!" then you get it.

Yes, that's it.

And yes, it's too easy for you only because it was indescribably difficult for Christ.

This is the gospel. This is the theology of Mark, and of all the biblical writers.

It's Always Been About Grace

Can you see why making the first section a lesson about divorce and remarriage is an exercise in missing the point? Can you see why turning Christ's hard sayings to the rich young ruler into the normal salvation invitation not only gets the point wrong, but backwards? Can you see how splitting apart these paragraphs spoils the beautiful message Mark intended?

Can you see how a blind beggar is the poster child for grace? Mark saved the best for last. And we now know the last shall be...

This is cross-centered, Christ-centered grace. The natural mind denies it. The carnal mind hates it. The unregenerate mind doesn't care about it at all.

But to us who belong to Jesus, this gospel of grace is the power of God. It is a treasury for our joys, a warehouse for our needs, a shelter in our storms, a power in our weakness, a guide for our steps, and a comfort in our sorrows. No religion offers it. No philosophy conceived it. No mind can plumb its depths. It flows eternally from the heart of God and will never lose its power.

This grace is the gift of God, paid by Christ, and poured out within the believing heart by the Holy Spirit.

Open your heart and let yourself fall forever into the everlasting arms of omnipotent, faithful, better-than-you-realize, unspeakably good, matchless, amazing grace.

May your breakthroughs to grace grow ever more glorious as you head toward that golden shore where you will one day step into a stupefying inheritance of future grace blessings.

> When my spirit, clothed Immortal,
> Wings its flight to reams of day,
> This my song, through endless ages,
> "Jesus led me all the way."
> *(Fanny J. Crosby, 1875)*

Worksheet

Using the bonus chapters above, fill in this chart with your observations and comments on Mark 10. Highlight the two paragraphs where grace is actually on display.

	Title & Verses	What Happened		Thoughts & reflections about grace and life
1		The Need for Grace, vv. 1-12	The Pharisees as a question of Jesus… he shows them they might be "lawful," but they're still sinning.	I can be doing everything right, according to the law, and still be unrighteous in God's sight. Even at my best, I still fall short and still desperately need God's grace. GRACE FAIL
2		The Attitude of Grace, vv. 13-16		 GRACE FAIL

3	The Antithesis of Grace, vv. 17-22		GRACE FAIL
4	The Origin of Grace, vv. 23-27		GRACE FAIL
5	The Cost-Benefit Analysis of Grace, vv. 28-31		GRACE FAIL
6	The True Cost of Grace, vv. 32-34	Jesus predicts his death and resurrection	

7	Blindness to Grace, vv. 35-45		GRACE FAIL
8	The Example of Grace, vv. 46-52		

Bonus Chapter 4

HOW TO BE SAVED

Are You Saved?

Perhaps, as you've read *Grace Breakthrough*, you realize you've never been saved. You're a church-going person, you're a good person, you're a God-loving person, maybe, but you're not a saved person. In fact, the language about being saved or born again makes you jittery.

I used the word *saved* on purpose. The Bible uses it all the time, so it's legit. Plus, it's weird enough to catch people's attention.

If you've reached this point in *Grace Breakthrough* and the study guide, you've read about who Christ is, and what he has done. You don't need any more teaching. Now, it's time to tie the knot.

As we do that, there are truths to be believed, a gift to be received, and a choice to be made.

Now let's hurry up and make your salvation official.

Truths To Be Believed

Without Christ, you were a moral train wreck. As good as you might be, you could never reverse the brokenness and fallenness inside you. You are a sinner from a long line of sinners and, as such, find yourself alienated from God and his love. Do you believe this?

You were, in fact, so messed up, that no amount of good works

> *For all have sinned and fall short of the glory of God, (Romans 3:23)*
> *All we like sheep have gone astray; We have turned, every one, to his own way; And the LORD has laid on Him the iniquity of us all. (Isaiah 53:6)*

could restore your relationship to God. No religion, no payment, no sacrifice, no achievement, no ritual. No one can ever live up to God's standards in their own power or fix themselves up to be acceptable to God. Do you believe this?

But God loves you and sent Jesus to reconcile you back to himself. Jesus was God's Son. Jesus died on the Cross and rose again. When he died on the Cross he died for you.

What this mean is God reached inside you long before you were ever born. He collected every sin, every failure, every evil, every dark thought, every hatred, lie, lust, and selfishness and removed that all from you. He transferred all your sins to Christ. And then he punished Christ for your sins instead of punishing you. Christ paid your penalty. He died the death you deserved. This was all God's work, God's love, and God's grace. The only thing you contributed were your sins. Do you believe this?

A Gift To Be Received

> For the wages of sin is death, but the gift of God is eternal life in Christ Jesus our Lord. (Romans 6:23)
>
> Being justified as a gift by His grace through the redemption which is in Christ Jesus. (Romans 3:24, NASB)

Because of what Jesus did on the Cross, God holds out a gift to you today. It is absolutely free; that's why it's called a gift. You can't earn it and don't deserve it. But God offers you a gift anyway. Are you willing to receive it?

What is the gift? It is everything Jesus is and brings into your soul. It is the gift of eternal life. It is the gift of Christ living in you. It is the gift of forgiveness of sins. It is the gift of justification, reconciliation, redemption, and all the wonders of being in Christ. It is the gift of a new start, with a new power, and a new identity. It is the gift of heaven, sure and guaranteed. Of all the big deals in your life, there is no deal as big and beautiful as the gift of salvation. Are you willing to receive Christ and his wonderful gift?

A Choice To Be Made

Are you willing to make the choice of faith alone in Christ alone? Notice, I said *willing*. I didn't say *ready*. Most people don't feel ready. But if you're willing, that's all it takes. It means God has made you ready.

If you're willing to be saved right now, then just tell God. Here is a sample prayer you might pray to him, following an ABC pattern. This is your choice.

> Believe on the Lord Jesus Christ, and you will be saved. (Acts 16:31)
>
> Therefore, having been justified by faith, we have peace with God through our Lord Jesus Christ, (Romans 5:1)

Dear God,

I ADMIT I need you. I have lived by my own ideas and strength, but it's not enough. I admit I have broken your laws. I admit I have sinned. I have let you down. I've even let myself down. I cannot reach you, and could never do enough to deserve salvation. I am a sinner, and I need you. I admit it God.

God I BELIEVE that Jesus is my way to you. I believe he is your Son. I believe he died on the Cross and rose again. I believe he did this for me, to cleanse my sins and make me acceptable in your sight. Only Jesus can save me. I'm not sure how it all works, but I'm telling you, God, right now, that I am believing in Jesus.

So right now I CHOOSE to receive Jesus as my Savior. I receive your gift. I choose to trust him as my Only Hope, for salvation, for heaven, for forgiveness, and for all the new labels I will find in him. I receive the gift of Christ and all he brings. I'm asking you right now, because of Jesus, God please save me, forgive me, and make me your own forever.

I pray in Jesus' name,
Amen.

If you prayed that prayer, God heard you. He has never turned anyone away. And you will belong to him forever. Tell a close friend, small group member, or pastor about what you've just done. If you don't have one, find a great group of believers to be part of.

God loves you and so do I.

I pray God's Grace Breakthrough will be strong in you all your days.

Now to Him who is able to keep you from stumbling, And to present you faultless Before the presence of His glory with exceeding joy, To God our Savior, Who alone is wise, Be glory and majesty, Dominion and power, Both now and forever.
Amen.
(Jude 1:24, 25)

Keep in Touch

Website: www.maxgrace.com
Twitter: www.twitter.com/BillGiovannetti
Facebook: www.facebook.com/PastorBillG

Please look for all the books in the *GRACE RESET* series:
Grace Intervention
*Grace Rehab**
*Grace Breakthrough**
*Grace Renovation (2017)**

(*Companion Study Guide Available)

www.ingramcontent.com/pod-product-compliance
Lightning Source LLC
Chambersburg PA
CBHW071303040426
42444CB00009B/1857